My Diary of Doorstep Delights

My Diary of
Doorstep Delights

by
Jillian Thorne

ryelands

First published in Great Britain in 2011

British Library Cataloguing-in-Publication Data
A CIP record for this title is available from the British Library

ISBN 978 1 906551 30 8

RYELANDS
Halsgrove House,
Ryelands Business Park,
Bagley Road, Wellington, Somerset TA21 9PZ
Tel: 01823 653777   Fax: 01823 216796
email: sales@halsgrove.com

Part of the Halsgrove group of companies
Information on all Halsgrove titles is available at: www.halsgrove.com

Printed in Italy by Grafiche Flaminia

Please may I introduce myself?

My name is Jillian Thorne. I was born and brought up in Wellington in Somerset and attended Bishop Fox's Grammar School for Girls at Taunton and the College of St Matthias at Bristol. After a thirty year career in Primary Schools in Kingston-Upon-Thames and Barnes in Surrey and Exeter and Kingskerswell in Devon I chose to take early retirement to discover the essence of freedom and peace and to indulge my passion for wild flowers. This little book is the fruition of my amateur attempts to capture their elusive and fragile beauty during those initial and blessed days.

I so enjoyed my time in Surrey. I will never forget the first view of the River Thames from Richmond Hill and walking beside it through gardens of pink cherry blossom. I thought I was in heaven when I strolled along dells of highly scented azaleas and rhododendrons in vibrant dazzling colours in the Savill Gardens in Windsor Great Park. Any free time in that superb tree-covered county was spent exploring the countryside, its many attractive towns, villages, stately houses and gardens. Its list of delights was endless and its proximity to the thrills of London provided everything one could wish for in those far-off heady days. Hampton Court Palace grounds became my garden for all seasons and latterly driving around Richmond Park to Barnes throughout the year became my twice daily joy.

Going to live by the sea fulfilled my next ambition and allowed me to settle back in the South West and live with coastal and moorland scenery on my doorstep. The garden at Dartington Hall then became my special place. It is a sanctuary away from the busy world, which in my youth I loved, but now in later life I leave for others to inhabit.

During the intervening years I have sadly witnessed the disappearance of many areas of wild flowers and feel enormous concern that what is left of the countryside is being turned into an adventure playground and a repository for litter. If only everyone could respect and treasure our glorious landscapes with their delicate and beautiful plant life!

"Almost anything that you do will seem insignificant, but it is very important that you do it."

Mahatma Gandhi

Taking Risks

To laugh is to risk seeming foolish.

To weep is to risk seeming sentimental.

To reach out for another risks involvement.

To expose your feelings risks rejection.

Open your dreams to the world and you'll risk ridicule.

Love and you'll risk not being loved in return.

Go forward with the odds against you and you'll risk failure.

But the greatest hazard of all is to risk nothing.

He who avoids these risks does nothing, has nothing, becomes nothing.

He will not feel, will not learn, love or grow.

He'll be a slave who has forfeited his freedom.

Brace yourself, look up, take your risks, be free!

Gill Lea.

When I first read and re-read this poem its sentiments spoke to me and penetrated my mind. I now take the risk of sharing my love and joy with you...

As the year unfolds I find myself making pilgrimages to all those places that reveal their seasonal wonders. The sight of the first Spring blooms has always made my heart feel like bursting. As I wandered freely here and there discovering the glories of each month and trying to capture their amazing forms with photographs, drawings or watercolours, I decided to record my thoughts and feelings so that these visual delights, sounds and scents would forever remain in my memory.

*"If I had but two loaves of bread
I would sell one and buy hyacinths —
for they would feed my soul."*

The Koran

JANUARY

Jan 1st

An explosion of fireworks signalled the beginning of a new year as Big Ben tolled its deep sonorous twelve chimes. Now there is so much to look forward to. The days are lengthening and new life is emerging. My resolution is to make sure that I don't miss any of its delights.

Jan 11th

The blue sky and sunshine beckoned me to my favourite garden at Dartington, to see what this January had so far produced. The overnight frost had melted into sparkling water droplets glazing the lawns and festooning the dainty branches of the trees. Winter jasmine grew by the gateway and early purple irises hugged the stone wall of the Great Hall, as if hiding from the cold. The first of the pale mauve and delicately wrapped petals of the early crocus had pushed through the grass under the cherries. A good covering of snowdrops had appeared through the crusty soil of the bank to display their drooping heads in reverence to yet another year!

Jan 24th

On arriving at Dartington again today I had the most wonderful welcome by an unseen reveller. I waited for a long time to see what bird could be emitting such a loud and glorious song. I can only guess it was a thrush by the power and perfection of its joyful call. Many more pale purple crocus adorned the wet grass with their genteel and erect form and there was now an abundance of snowdrops on the beautiful bank. Each week something new makes an appearance. It is amazing! A few inquisitive aconites were peeping reluctantly through the moss above the tiltyard, their yellow petals like so many fairy lights dotting the way. The scent from the bushes of Winter box that are all over the garden pervaded the air and the witch hazels, mahonia and Winter honeysuckle added their special perfumes.

Jan 26th

It was gloriously sunny today so I decided to head out to look for snowdrops in the countryside. I first drove to Ashprington and East Cornworthy, stopping to admire the stunning view of the River Dart as it wound its way through the lush Devon landscape to the sea at Dartmouth, and there they were hiding in the woods and hedges. In the next village of Dittisham they were massed on the sloping lawns behind some of the pretty cottages. I wonder what it would be like to live in that quiet, scenic hamlet with a sail-boat moored on the meandering river?

Jan 31st

The need to escape to the silence and beauty of the countryside has brought me to moorland on the road to Manaton. It is the 'Roland Hilder' time of the year when the green and brown tracery of the tree branches stretch unclothed heavenward. I love this still resting period when the greatest season of hope awaits.

"The sense of existence is the greatest happiness"

Benjamin Disraeli

FEBRUARY

Feb 9th

I had been told that there were also snowdrops at Staverton so as the sun was shining I decided to take a peep. What a delight! For miles around the village they clustered in the hedges and filled the churchyard. Along the river bank there were thousand upon thousand more looking like snowdrifts beside the swollen, rushing water. My joy was unbounded. They seem to pop up from nowhere after a dull Winter, exciting the soul.

Feb 10th

There was a sharp frost this morning which made the air cool and clear. At Dartington Hall Gardens I sat on a wooden seat on a green lush bank overlooking the grounds. It was covered with flowers. Purple and white crocus opened their giving petals to the bumble bees and revealed their bright orange stigmas and stamens. Tiny wild daffodils and clumps of dainty snowdrops nodded their heads in the breeze. The sunshine picked up the texture of the green velvety moss that carpeted the slope. A blackbird rummaged for food in the undergrowth nearby and robins and chaffinches sang in the trees above. What luxury! What bliss!

Feb 16th

Last night I enjoyed the company of a good friend, but by late evening we discovered that there had been a heavy fall of snow. Everything looked so clean and beautiful wrapped in what appeared to be a soft white, feathered counterpane! This morning the sun shone in a clear blue sky and everywhere looked stunning under its sparkling cover. I walked to the seafront gardens – their seats now adorned with soft white cushions – and onto Cockington where the bare branches of the trees were etched and the shining camellia leaves were laden with crystalline flakes. It looked like a photograph from a Winter calendar. All was silent apart from the steady dripping and crackling of the thaw where the sun was penetrating.

In the park, however, there was a different scene. The holidaying children were excitedly trundling their toboggans and metal trays up the slopes and screaming with delight as they sped down through the groups of their waiting, watching, chattering mothers and all the many dogs that they had brought with them were barking with enthusiasm.

In the quiet gardens surrounding the church the magnolia flowers now looked like large white light bulbs and the delicate branches of the acer were glinting with drops of ice. It was a morning to remember.

Feb 24th

St Matthias' Day! I took a leisurely stroll around Killerton Gardens which are so wonderful in the fresh days of early Spring. Daffodils, primroses, crocus and snowdrops clothed the hillsides. A tall pink magnolia was in full bloom and a white one nearby was just beginning to flower.

Feb 28th

Today I strayed a little further away from home and thought I was in a dream world sitting on a seat beside rippling waters of the lake and gazing at the undulating lawns where vast drifts of purple and white crocus carpeted the slopes with their beauty. It was magical in those grounds that lead down to the large and very grand crenellated towers of the yellow stone Forde Abbey in Somerset.

"Thanks to the human heart by which we live.
Thanks to its tenderness, its joys and fears.
To me the meanest flower that blooms can give
thoughts that do often lie too deep for tears."

William Wordsworth

MARCH

March 1st

St David's Day! I have just taken a drive over the moors. When I set off the weather was cold and clear. I discovered a lovely wooded road beside the rushing river at Spitchwick. I laughed when on the higher ground clouds gathered and I got caught in an unexpected blizzard. It was so pretty for many miles as the car was cocooned by white flakes swirling around in their ballet of ice.

March 4th

There was a bright start to the day, so I decided it may be enjoyable to drive to Overbecks at Bolt Head, Salcombe. As I arrived I was greeted by a pair of robins that put their heads on one side, as if to say 'Hello, what are you doing here?' As I walked into the grounds I was amazed by the view. Could there be anywhere more beautiful, I wondered? The scent of orange blossom in the conservatory brought back memories of Cyprus in the Spring. The Union Jack was flying proudly from a white flagpole. This was a little corner of which one can be proud. The only sounds were the crashing of the waves on the shore, the wind rustling the branches of the trees and the songs of the birds. There were scented and pale primroses everywhere. I walked up a sloping path, passed through an archway and to my left was a glorious sight that almost took my breath away. A magnificent pink magnolia with long outstretched limbs covered in cup-like blossoms and fat candle-like buds was at its most perfect. On closer inspection I could see the drops of rain adorning the thick, waxy magenta petals and pretty green lichen encrusting the branches which looked as if they were very, very old. Beyond this splendid sight was the blue sea and rugged coastline of this as yet, unspoiled area of South Devon.

March 9th

Just inside the quadrangle at Dartington Hall there were clouds of palest pink blossom in each corner. I tried to paint the first few fritillaries and blue anemone blanda. A blackbird sang to me all the while. His song signalled new life and warmth and heralded these wondrous days for which we have waited for so long. There were daffodils everywhere – in gardens, in hedges, on roadsides and on roundabouts. They trumpet in the best season of the year and brighten the dullest day with this splash of sunshine gold.

March 10th

I drove over Dartmoor to the Garden House today. It was a long way, but worth it. Another pink magnolia caught my eye. The setting was idyllic. It stood by an old, stone, ivy-clad, slate-roofed hut, beside a quietly flowing stream. The pink buds were poised and positioned heavenward, as if stretching out of their old grey fur coats to embrace the blue sky above, rejoicing at last to be throwing off the trappings of Winter. Lovecombe cottage stood nearby, surrounded with clumps of white daisies, daffodils and pink primroses. It nestled cosily into the hillside. What a lovely name – expressly deep contentment!

Cotehele was my next 'port-of-call'. It exuded antiquity. You will love it if you go there – the swathes of daffodils, the mounds of primroses, the violets near the stone gateway, the mossy bank, the orchard of apple trees and mistletoe, the white doves and the view of the river and the viaduct and the boats! I chatted to two pretty children. They each held a magnolia bud and were stroking them lovingly as they told me they were little mice! It was all so perfect. I didn't want to leave!

March 14th

Well, I have been searching for country lanes and there were plenty in the Teign Valley. There the river flowed through banks and fields of gold daffodils – all the cottage gardens were full of every variety of narcissus. Spring is here! I was trying to find silence and solitude. There my only company was that of bleating lambs, singing song birds and rippling streams. I find peace in such places and at such times and that is very important to me.

I walked through the glades of native dancing daffodils at Dunsford Woods and sat to gaze upon that beautiful scene. How lucky we are to have such places on our doorstep!

March 16th

My journey took me up to Dulverton and onto Exmoor on a bleak wet afternoon. The brown bracken was a deep tan colour, but the old hawthorns looked like black witches in the rain, dotted all over the moorland, stretching out their gnarled arms and menacing accusatory fingers and groaning at the weather!

March 18th

Today I visited Bicton Gardens with its banks of pale yellow and pink primroses and wild daffodils. Groups of white narcissi with orange centres were at their best looking so elegant as they decked the path. The pair of white swans looked so regal gliding along the still lake with their clear reflections. They were accompanied by a pair of dull feathered mallards, beautiful in their own way and to each other no doubt, but they lacked the grace and distinction possessed by the swans – such is life!

March 24th

It was a warm sunny Spring day as I re-visited Killerton. The daffodils and primroses on the banked hillside garden lawns were wondrous and interspersed with groups of bright pink cyclamen. Here and there were large rhododendrons and the occasional patch of wood anemones. The early tortoiseshell butterflies were fluttering around and the birds were pairing in flight.

Large bumble bees hummed past searching the ground for nectar-laden succulence. A robin serenaded me from a nearby tree. A thrush was foraging.

Yesterday I enjoyed strolling down the beautiful flower-strewn drive at Greenway House where the magnolia reigned supreme and the humble primroses kissed the feet of the large stately beech.

March 28th

Things have changed at Dartington Hall. The white cherries are now perfect with their virginal flower petals and their brown buds lightly touched with smears of pink from which their bright yellowy green leaves were emerging. Beauty, love and joy filled my being as I dwelt on their magnificence. Further around the garden there were groups of white anemones, pink cyclamen and nodding purple and white fritillaries.

"April – the angel of the months."

Vita Sackville-West

APRIL

April 3rd

The Easter weekend brought magnificent weather and all the Spring primroses, daffodils, anemones, violets and celandines suddenly seemed to bloom together in celebration. The sight of a circle of these wondrous flowers embedded in soft green moss around the rim of the font at Bradford-on-Tone church in Somerset was exquisite. Their scent, delicacy and freshness overwhelmed me. I love to visit churches on Easter Saturday afternoons when I know they will be beautifully decorated.

April 5th

The air was warm, the sun bright and the sky cloudless blue as I surveyed the sea-front gardens this morning. They were filled with colourful tulips and pansies and scented polyanthus and wallflowers.

April 13th

I sat under the boughs of a pure white cherry tree in blossom. The bees hummed as they busily visited the centre of each flower – they hadn't the time or inclination to notice the shape and beauty of the overhanging branches, each ending in a cluster of perfection. The clear blue sky above added sunshine, clarity, shadow and shape to one of Spring's real treasures at Dartington Hall. A bride could not wish for a more natural and lovely canopy. The surrounding wide expanses of newly mown lawns, sprinkled with white daisies added a grandeur to the horizontal dimension and

scented the air. The mossy roots provided me with an ideal perch as the sun warmed my skin and relaxed my body. The petals fell all around like confetti in the light breeze. Such a place gives happiness to many.

How can I begin to describe the bank above the tiltyard? I viewed grassy slopes covered with patches of pale, bright centred, eager faced, gently perfumed primroses, stretching up in determination to enjoy the warmth of such a wonderful day. Pink cyclamen added highlights of cerise and bluebells hung on erect or slightly stooping stems nodding in the whispering air. Purple violets peeped out and white and purple fritillaries shook their heads in disbelief at the beauty all around. Yellow celandines reflected the sun's glow, their shining petals opened by its heat. The green density of leaf shapes and shadows made a restful carpet and gave life and prominence to these natural gems. The white daisies shared the day with their Spring companions and the wood anemones added a delicacy and daintiness as they danced in the breeze – real wind flowers. I was in heaven. Nothing could have been more perfect.

There were more hidden corners in this garden – had anyone else espied the drift of bright cyclamen and white wood anemones gracing the feet of a sturdy fir? They nestled comfortably and happily together spreading outwards to embrace a sea of bluebells. A gathering of purple violets was almost hidden under a dense cover of foliage – daring to look out to see what was going on in their little backwater. They are shy but interesting, simple but knowing. I looked at them and enjoyed their glorious perfume. They spoke to me of the sensitivity of life. I treasured their existence but was afraid for them. Things so small and seemingly unimportant will not survive if not given space, consideration and worth. Man with his often unseeing and uncaring attitude could so easily eliminate such jewels.

Moving on I discovered glades of pheasants eye narcissi which I adore, cream erythroniums which are another favourite, blue and white anemone blanda which are delightful, blue, white and pink bells, primroses, periwinkle and speedwell. Can you imagine anything more sublime? Uneven stone steps sprinkled still with the leaves of last year led to a secluded seat which was lined with pink azaleas and overhung by branches of magnolia in which a robin sang. Maybe you will understand why this place is so important...?

April 28th

I feel tired after walking up and down so many steep slopes yesterday! Coleton Fishacre peaks at this time of year with sweeps of bluebells and white wild garlic combining to make a magnificent sight as they lead your eye across to the sea. There is nothing more heart warming and magical than to see large expanses of wild flowers growing on the sloping hillside.

I visited Greenway House in the afternoon as it is always glorious at bluebell time. They cover the ground as it drops away to the river below. I sat at the top most viewpoint where the large mature trees were just bursting into leaf. A few ornamental cherries were flowering and giving a pink glow to the scene. Moored sail-boats were on the water, a heron flew sedately past and the occasional pleasure launch chugged along extolling the fascinations of the Dart and its well-known inhabitants. All around were cinquefoils, cuckoo flowers, wild strawberries, primroses, violets, blue bugle and so many more of nature's treasures.

April 30th

I went exploring today to see and discover places that were new to me. I had a lovely drive over the moors and ventured down to the Torpoint Ferry where I crossed the River Tamar. I found my way to the parkland at Mount Edgcumbe and took a stroll overlooking Plymouth Sound and Drake's Island. Watching the Brittany Ferries boat arrive brought back many happy memories. I was fortunate enough to see a nuclear submarine leave the harbour. It slid quietly and surreptitiously along like some black whale. The sea and sky were a brilliant blue as I took in the coastal scenery of that part of Cornwall. Finally I made my first visit to Antony. I met Lady Carew-Pole picking some azaleas and remembered that I had briefly seen her before when she was Princess Anne's lady-in-waiting when I took the children to give her a cheque for her favourite charity. I walked through the bluebells and rested on a wooden bench overlooking the Lynher estuary. It was a grand end to a most interesting day.

*"Flowers reflect the human search for meaning.
Does not each one of us, no matter how our life has gone,
ache to have a life as beautiful and true to
itself as that of a flower."*

Princess Grace of Monaco

MAY

May 2nd

I had hoped to visit Tuscany in early May; that somehow didn't materialize so I decided to ramble around England instead.

The day began well as it was a bright and sunny morning and the new fresh green leaves of the lime trees in the churchyard cheered me as I looked out of the window.

I drove to Shaldon along the coastal road passing a group of purple orchids growing on a bank. The River Teign spanned by Shaldon Bridge was calm, blue and tranquil beset with a multitude of small boats bathing in the sunshine. Every time I pass that way I marvel at the view. White and pink flowering cherries lined the hill as I left Teignmouth.

At East Lambrook Manor, which was our first port-of-call, there was a scent of orange blossom in the air. It was heady and powerful and came from an insignificant climbing plant with small waxy flowers. The pretty soft pink dainty cherry by the gate was intertwined with the lovely early pink honeysuckle.

Barrington Court was peaceful with an abundance of wallflowers, bluebells, daisies and wide open pastures. I heard the cuckoo call and as it was the first time I had heard it this year I had to run a little way – to bring me luck! There was a lovely splash of orange, yellow and pink poppies in the vegetable garden and the apple blossom in the orchard was a delight. Two ducks strolled companionably across the lawn.

I loved Tintinhull with its urns of white tulips. Deep blue ceanothus and purple wisteria hanging in delicate strands decorated the Elizabethan hamstone wall at Montacute.

We found a thatched cottage with uneven wooden floors and dark oak beams in which to have bed and breakfast. I liked its old and quaint ambience and its narrow creaking staircase. We had a pleasant walk around the grand lake at Stourhead with its temples, statues and grottos and admired the reflections of the green and yellow trees in its still waters. The geese on the lawns were for some unknown reason making a great commotion and the bells of the nearby church peeled out over the tranquillity of the evening.

May 3rd
Experiencing Stourhead lakeside in the early morning felt good and quite different. The bluebell woods along the roadside were a haze of blue forever and climbing the hillside. The density of their growth and the deepness of their colour was a sight to behold.

Last year I fell in love with a book about the new life given to Ashtree cottage, so as we were passing I thought to call. The owner was weeding and her pretty garden was edged with pink tulips that had opened wide to receive the sun's warmth.

On we went through stunning countryside of rolling hills and valleys, with beautiful beeches doing their best to line the way with welcome. There were bluebells at the sides of the road and cherry and apple blossom around every corner! We drove along Paradise Lane and finally arrived at Heaven's Gate. Well, we have found them in this life – do you think we will in the next?

There are some extremely attractive villages in Wiltshire. We stopped in one where nearly every house was an architectural dream, and there was such a variety of styles, charm and character. They were small and regularly proportioned with unassuming but delightful gardens.

It felt like high Summer with the temperature reaching 80°F when we arrived at Lacock Abbey. The lawns on two sides were superb with their newly cut stripes. The others had patches of wild flowers growing in them which I thought was a lovely touch. Some older, velvety irises grew by the ancient stone wall. The meadows all around were knee-deep in buttercups and the globular seed heads of dandelions – one puff of wind would send them flying to who knows where. The cows rested lazily in the water meadows.

That evening we stayed at Tetbury in a house with a charming garden. I sat in the evening sunshine. The birds chattered all around and I was surrounded by blue and white bells and the daintiest and prettiest collection of red, pink, cerise and purple anemones. That town was full of character and that special corner near St Michael's church was particularly interesting. The jumble of steeply sloping roof

tiles was alluring. The old stooping apple trees – guardians of the garden – were flowering. A clump of bright yellow shining kingcups grew by a small pond. Three old weather-worn wooden seats hid in sturdy arbours under the shelter of the dry Cotswold stone walls. A yellow rose was climbing in through an open bedroom window. The owners of this garden exuded a quite calm and grace that befitted their friendly and beautiful house. It was a wonderful retreat.

May 5th

Westonbirt Arboretum in one word – bluebells! Glade upon glade of deep, shimmering, scented blue! Amazing!

May 8th

Well, hello again! The sky was an intense blue and the sun poured its warmth over me. Early May is the most perfect time in England. Birds of all kinds were carolling merrily, the trees were in new leaf and there were flowers and blossom everywhere. Here among the green meadows, elegant trees and Spring blossoms I felt happy. Stillness, rest, calm, isolation, tranquillity, beauty and orderliness were my gifts for today. Yes, I was at Dartington Hall!

May 10th

Sitting on a high point near Start Point lighthouse I looked back at the sweep of a yellow and blue carpet stretching down to a calm blue sea, where little ripples of white foam played around the rocks at the base of the slopes of bluebells and primroses. It was a scintillating and scented sight. The roads leading there had been adorned with stitchwort, bluebells and campions. I think they are some of the loveliest lanes in South Devon.

The thrift and sea campions occupied part of the beach at Slapton Sands and moved me to photograph them. The seascapes in this area are remarkable. I walked down to Mattiscombe and as I lay in the warm sun on the edge of the cliff the blue clear water glinted like so many flashing 'Tinkerbells'!

J. THORNE

May 19th

I set off across the moors for another day out and stopped beside the River Dart at Huccaby, where in the Autumn the water was wild. Today it was splashing merrily and calmly around the rocks on its sparkling way, while the dipper, with its white throat bounced and flew up and down the stream. The bright green spreading sycamore and the pale orange copper beech bowed their branches in homage. The brilliance of the gorse on the moors was astounding – quite the yellowest of yellows. The trees everywhere looked wonderful. The variety of green shapes and the clean freshness of the leaves and the sap-green of the beeches in particular was mesmerising.

The Garden House – oh! ah! A mass of wild and garden plants with views through circles and arches of wisteria and towering white trees laden with blossom into which clematis had climbed and was hanging in garlands. The narrow paths were lined with pink, orange and yellow azaleas and nooks and crannies were packed with every plant imaginable. This was a painter's paradise – an embroidery of colour, shape and texture. A carpet of white, pale and dark pink stars pushed their way through the soil like gentians in the mountains once the snow has melted – rhodohypoxis baurii. This was a transport of delight. Every corner revealed something new and beautiful and every vista was a dream of creation. Old stone walls were encrusted with white and purple wisteria and paths were edged with orange poppies. It was a secret, magical place surrounded by a high stone wall like a protecting arm of comfort. The garden nestled below the head and face of the house, enchanting all who entered. There were stone steps, grassy curved paths, mosses and ferns peeping out from cracks. Here a large red poppy, there hedges,

ruins, thatched roofs, clipped yews, blowzy peonies and a spread of lacy white hydrangea.

Lovecombe cottage was now surrounded by a bank of pink campions, bluebells, buttercups and bright blue alkanet. The air was warm in this sheltered place. White butterflies hovered and alighted on the blooms. The cherries and magnolias had long since lost their blossoms and were in full leaf. The ivy-clad shed, the trickling stream, the cow parsley, the goose grass, the white deadnettle, the herb robert – there was no mistaking it was mid-May. This spot was like a botanical Noah's Ark. There seemed to be two or more of every kind of plant, collected, contained and closed off from the rest of the world, preserved for all time to show what England's beauty had been like.

"Earth's crammed with heaven."

Elizabeth Barrett Browning

JUNE

June 9th

I sat by a fast flowing stream on an old wooden bench, surrounded by a paradise of flowers in the heart of the South Hams near Kellerton. It is a tiny village of cottages, old stone walls topped with daisies, ferns and yellow Tom Thumb. Beside the water were white arum lilies and yellow flag irises. The nearest wall was smothered in purple campanula, red and white valerian, pink and white daisies and ivy-leaved toadflax. The apple orchard was awash with buttercups, cow parsley and campions. It was bright and sunny but rather breezy. I had intended to join friends in Brittany but the strong winds made me turn back. I am envying their companionship, the fresh air and the beautiful beaches, but I am in peaceful stunning England at its best, so that can't be bad.

June 12th

Today I visited the grounds of Castle Drogo. I had forgotten about the circular croquet lawn surrounded by closely clipped yew hedging. The wind was very cold. It felt more like February than June. Well cut hedges were also a feature of the sloping parterres. A deep red velvety rose grew and flowered among the scented azaleas. I loved the crunch of my footsteps on the gravel paths and the view of the hills beyond. The canopied entrances to the garden were impressive with a tree in each corner its branches trained over metal arches. The curved herbaceous borders surrounding the rose garden were filled with yellows, oranges, blues, pinks and purples – the outstanding plants today being the almost unnatural blue, four-petalled Himalayan poppies. The roses had been severely pruned and were not yet in flower.

A yew-hedged terrace was above a slope of rhododendrons and the view over the moorland and soft green countryside was vast and interspersed with gently wooded hills and a patchwork of fields leading to higher peaks. It was all so well managed and peaceful as we would like everywhere to be.

Mr Drewe's path led through a wood overlooking a deep ravine, at the bottom of which flowed a splashing, gurgling river. A myriad of birds darted hither and thither. It reminded me of being in the hills of Provence, except the slopes were cloaked in ash, beeches and English oak, rather than mimosa, pines, chestnuts and cork oak. Apart from the birds and the river it was silent. There were conveniently placed wooden benches at viewing points – all so civilized and splendid! I feel lucky to be born at a time when these lovely places can be shared and are well-cared for thanks to the National Trust. There is a certain graciousness about vast well-cut lawns and stately tree-lined drives. They imbue a sense of serenity, which is a priceless gift.

Foxgloves are the proud sentinels of this time of year.

The nearby village was Drewsteignton. The church tower flew the flag of St George and all around were thatched cottages edged with the flowers of Summer – campanulas, daisies, pinks, geraniums, lupins, rock roses, aquilegia, pansies and poppies. Roses, honeysuckle, wisteria and clematis climbed the wall and pink and white valerian added a natural touch watching all passers-by.

I next popped over to Rosemoor, the Royal Horticultural Society's garden. I rested in the wooden thatched Summer house in an area created to represent a cottage garden. The path was lined with standard roses and pots of fuchsias, daisies and pansies. A red rose grew either side and all around were lupins, geraniums, aubretia, sage, delphiniums, Californian poppies and a wonderful group of yellow and pale pink foxgloves.

In Lady Anne's garden two mature trees – one ash one oak – provided a lovely vista of the house with lawns and flower beds beckoning one forth. The cascades of white and pale and deep pink briar roses were particularly fine and their scent was heady in the warmth of this sheltered spot.

I loved it in the garden where clematis and roses climbed together, their flowers intertwining in a most natural way. The lake was very pretty too with purple and white irises, pink and yellow water lilies and red and yellow candelabra primulas – I must go to Giverny! I ended the day by walking along the sandy beach at Instow then resting and viewing the boat-filled estuary from the comfort of the terrace at the Commodore Hotel which is my favourite hostelry in North Devon!

June 14th

All the flower-bedecked cottages looked so attractive nestling into the combe at Slapton village. I took my first swim of the year on the sandy beach at Mattiscombe. It felt gorgeous!

Can you imagine how my senses reeled when on the way home I espied a field of blood-red poppies growing amongst the corn, somewhere between Harbertonford and Totnes. I stopped in a lay-by and walked through them taking photos and marvelling at that sea of scarlet!

June 16th

I thought I would make my way to East Portlemouth on this glorious June day. The sweep of the road bending into the village of South Pool was picturesque, lined with cottages edged with flowers and cobblestones. As I rounded the corner there was a pink-washed cottage with a red rose climbing to the top of its gable end. A stream trickled by and an old lady was sitting outside her home enjoying the sun. Along the creek the tide was in and two white swans commandeered the island by the bridge. Stepping stones crossed the stream, a pied-wagtail hopped along the bank, swifts swooped low over the water and a heron paddled by an old rowing boat. Under a honeysuckle hanging wantonly over an old stone wall there was a peephole into a garden where two ducks were wandering over a daisy-strewn lawn. What a fabulous existence they had! A yacht was moored in the deep water around the bend, the sky was clear and blue and the green fields sloped down to the edge of the water. Cattle were browsing, bees were humming, birds were twittering and water was lapping around the stones. What a fabulous existence I was enjoying at that moment!

I next drove along the narrow lane beside the creek and stopped where the road widened to house a slipway. White and blue sail-boats with flags jangling on their masts rested calmly on the azure waters which were contrasted with the emerald wheat growing on the hillside beyond. Quite a cool breeze rippled the estuary. A man in navy blue was repairing his tender and two small rowing boats nudged each other from time to time.

Eventually I reached Sunny Cove. The water was icy, but I needed three dips to keep cool! The flowers on the cliff were so pretty – white daisies, cerise cranesbill, blue scabious, honeysuckle and wild roses. A boat was moored off the beach all the afternoon, but eventually sailed away into the sunset.

June 19th

I travelled to Paris on Eurostar yesterday! I can't believe it! We are lucky enough to have a superb flat in a central position opposite Les Invalides. That building has recently been renovated and the walls and pillars are gleaming, as is the golden dome, topped by a cross. As I sat in the window at the end of a sunny day the Eiffel Tower was to my left and the Sacré Coeur was across the Seine and on the other side to my right. This afternoon we walked in the vast and impressive grounds at Fontainebleau and this evening we had a stroll on the grass in front of the magnificent black and gold gates of Les Invalides and over the Alexander Bridge spanning the Seine, where numerous bateaux-mouches were plying up and down. The pillars of each corner of the bridge were impressive with shining gold statuettes on top. We walked up the Champs Elysées, past fountains and gardens of white flowers and the rest of the world, until it grew dark and the Arc de Triomphe was silhouetted against the pink glow of the setting sun.

June 20th

Today I visited Giverny – at last! I think any garden should be visited alone, but I did my best to ignore the other people and concentrate on the flowers! My immediate impression was that the ground had been carefully combed and the contents of a million seed packets had been sprinkled over it, resulting in plant growth with an amazing colour mix and height variation. I am sure it was at its best and most luxurious with poppies and geraniums in vibrant shades appearing beside standard and under arches of climbing roses of reds, pinks and yellows. Monet was fanatical about flowers as I am! I sat under an old apple tree and painted daubs of colour trying to invoke his spirit. Should think he would be horrified to see so many folk tramping over his beloved plot – but on the other hand he may be overjoyed to know that so many love flowers the way he did…?

June 21st

The longest day! I was in heaven! The rose garden at Parc du Bagatelle in the Bois de Boulogne was everything I had hoped for. There grew archways, pillars, standard cascading trees and low bushes of every colour and type of rose imaginable. The air was scented with their perfume. The beds were bordered with lawns and hedges of box. It was divine! The gardeners were busy dead-heading so that every specimen was perfect. I have never seen such an immaculate and magnificent garden.

Later in the day we explored Rodin's garden. The dome of Les Invalides stood over us like a guardian. The pretty newly-cleaned stone house with its arched windows sat elegantly behind the lawned white flower borders and circular pond. The outside world rushed by. There all was calm and lovers kissed and entwined on the stone benches and wooden seats amongst the statues.

June 23rd
Today we so enjoyed our walk through the Tuilleries gardens to the Pyramid and the Louvre taking a bus over the Seine past Notre-Dame to the Jardin des Plantes. Later we took another bus to the superb Luxembourg Palace gardens which were so stylishly laid out and were filled with Parisiennes having their lunch, sitting elegantly on the folding green metal seats. Sadly and finally we took the bus to Place Vaubin and on to the Gare du Nord. What a marvellous few days.

June 24th
We visited Polesden Lacey in Surrey on our way home from Paris. It was there that King George VI and Queen Elizabeth spent their honeymoon. Happy memories flooded over me as we walked under the rose arches and admired the borders of poppies, clematis and delphiniums.

It was dull and cool by the time we reached Mottisfont Abbey's walled garden in Hampshire – but that small area was a picture in pink, white and green. It was a symphony of foxgloves, roses and pinks – quite, quite magical.

We finished our travels in pursuit of the rose by visiting Barrington where the village was endowed with rose covered cottages and the Court had one particular white specimen climbing the hamstone wall.

This pretty song is poignant and seems to echo the poem about taking risks. I listened to it with interest.

The Rose

Some say love it is a river
That drowns the tender reed.
Some say love it is a razor
That leaves your soul to bleed.
Some say love it is a hunger –
An endless aching need
I say love it is a flower
And you its only seed.

It's the heart afraid of breaking
That never learns to dance.
It's the dream afraid of waking
That never takes a chance
It's the one who won't be taken
Who cannot seem to give
And the soul afraid of dying
That never learns to live.

When the night has been so lonely
And the road has been too long
When you think that love is only
For the lucky and the strong
Just remember in the Winter
Far beneath the bitter snow
Lies the seed that with the sun's love
In the Spring becomes the rose.

"To sit in the shade on a fine day and look upon verdure is the most perfect refreshment."

Jane Austen

JULY

July 2nd

Dunkery Beacon is one of my favourite viewing places. July is a good time to be there. Today a wonderful scene was set out below me. I could see the coastline of South Wales across the waters of the Bristol Channel, and the tree-covered hills and combes above Porlock and Bossington and the hedge-lined pastures and woodlands all around me. I was surrounded by purple, pink and white heather, green ferns and the leaves of the wortleberry. I was surprised to see the latter bearing their dark ripe berries and picked some to taste. I used to bring my mother here and we used to try and identify Nash lighthouse and Southerndown in the 'Promised Land' as the Welsh vicar of Selworthy church once said to her when we visited it for a flower festival. Every year I take a pilgrimage to this area and the Brendon Hills as the extensive and tall plants of spiky fireweed or rose-bay willow herb make an outstanding display set among the beech hedges which make this unspoilt part of Somerset look like one enormous garden.

July 14th

Today I walked by a canal from Powderham to Turf and back and enjoyed a companionable and thoughtful day discussing creativity and simplicity. The pink and delicate flowers of the blackberry were now flowering and many butterflies hovered over them making the most of their brief and beautiful lives.

July 15th

As I walked on the newly washed beach at Meadfoot the tide had prepared the sands for a new day and I pondered the ambition of a friend to write a book that people would treasure.

July 20th

I took a long walk around the headland of the pretty riverside village of Dittisham after having lunch on the terrace café. The sky was blue after the violent storms of the previous night. The green plums in the orchard were swelling and had a wonderful bloom. Dittisham used to be well-known for its plum trees, but now very few remain.

"Teach us delight in simple things."

Rudyard Kipling

AUGUST

August 5th

Yesterday I caught the boat from Dittisham to Dartmouth, walked to the castle and dangled my feet in the cool sea as I sat on a rock and ate a refreshing ice cream. It's what you do in the Summer holidays isn't it? In the evening I went over to Dartington Hall, and listened to the music coming from the windows of the Great Hall as it wafted across the quadrangle. I strolled through the garden to enjoy the purple, yellow and white herbaceous border which is always glorious in August.

Today I had lunch at The Pigs Nose at East Prawle and spent the afternoon at Sunny Cove watching the sun setting over the estuary at Salcombe. The view from East Portlemouth towards Kingsbridge is one of the wonders of the world.

Aug 11th

The weather was hot and sunny so I returned to East Portlemouth. I love it there. A gentle breeze brought down the temperature, lightly rippled the water and fluttered the flags. There was a good deal of activity with sailing boats tacking back and forth, a few motor boats passing by and many yachts moored with their owners sunning themselves on deck. Children were at the water's edge scooping up crabs and shrimps in their nets. Everyone seemed relaxed at play and happy. It was high Summer in South Devon.

"Earth laughs in flowers"

Ralph Waldo Emerson

SEPTEMBER

Sept 12th

The last time I sat admiring this wonderful view at Start Bay from the rocks near the lighthouse, the sloping cliffs were blue and yellow – being covered with bluebells and primroses. Today they are a golden brown as Autumn approaches and they are covered in bracken. The Summer bids us farewell. June and July and August brought some lovely days. It was grand to behold a blue calm sea with little white yachts dotting its surface and feel the warmth of the September sun. I thought the swallows may have already returned to Africa, but no, flying beside, around and above me there were dozens swooping and darting at top speed in order to feast on the multitude of airborne insects. They twittered faintly as they passed and with their dark backs, pale breasts and forked tails they flapped their wings excitedly and energetically giving me a startlingly beautiful display of aerobatics. A host of red admiral and black tipped white butterflies fluttered past too. Today they were all so active! The last few Summer flowers adorned the hedges especially honeysuckle, blue scabious and yellow toadflax and I saw blue chicory beside the road at Slapton Sands. The view as I came down the highway from Strete was breathtaking.

Sept 14th

I explored the Somerset Levels today. It is an area of flat wetland in contrast to the hills of the Blackdowns and the Quantocks and has its own special magic. It was criss-crossed with ditches, canals and roads lined with willows. I remembered once visiting it after heavy rain when the fields had become lagoons and the crooked pollarded trees were mirrored in the water. Today all the local artists were exhibiting their work in their cottages or village halls. Everyone I spoke to was so friendly and it made for a most interesting interlude.

The Autumn sunshine warmed the air as I strolled over the little bridge and through the arched gateway into the walled gardens full of enchantment at Barrington Court. I was pleased by the red, yellow and orange garden, delighted by the pink and purple borders, but entranced by the white garden as the heady scent of the climbing roses assailed my nostrils.

Sept 22nd

I felt the need to get away from it all so went out early and drove onto the moors. The expanse of rolling landscape let me breathe. The sun was bright and highlighted the deep red berries of the hawthorns and the brilliant orange berries of the rowans that were massed in thick bundles all over the shapely trees. I stopped by an old bridge over a trickling stream. The view through the wooden gateway of stone-walled fields and open moorland beyond was extremely peaceful. A bird sang from the gorse bush and a red admiral butterfly fluttered past.

Sept 28th

I was up very much earlier than usual and was able to observe more wonderful reflections as the dawn broke over the boat laden estuary of the River Teign and the sun rose in a large red globe over the red-filled sea at Dawlish Warren. I walked the sands and paddled in the gently lapping waters before many were awake – an extremely rare occurrence I must admit! Thoughts of life, freedom and peace of mind were circling in my head as the gulls circled in the air currents above!

"I would if I could, bring back into fashion the moon and the stars, the dawn and the sunset. I rarely hear anyone speak of them."

Max Ehrmann

OCTOBER

Oct 14th

The leaves were beginning to turn colour and the ground was strewn with beech nuts masts, acorns and pine needles at Dartington Hall. The banks were green again after the September rains and looked lush and content to rest for the Winter as they guarded and covered the sleeping abundance of life beneath. The occasional group of pink cyclamen penetrated the verdure and the tall, delicate stems of purple Autumn crocus added their seasonal beauty. A damp mouldering smell hung in the air.

Oct 19th

I made another early start in order to see the dawn break in streaks of pink and blue cloud. The lanes beckoned me onto the lower edge of the moor to rest at Spitchwick. There the leaves were swirling and fluttering around my head. The heavy dew on the grass sparkled in the sunshine. As I walked over it every droplet glittered in the fresh Autumnal morn. The river splashed along and was a background accompaniment to the chirping of the chaffinches, the trilling of the robins and the caw of the crows. A brown bracken-covered tor could be seen through the yellowing silver-barked birches and the blue sky gave cheer to the heart after so many grey days. The berries of the holly, hawthorn and rose were gleaming in the sun and lighting my way like beacons. How fortunate I am to be able to see these unbelievable sights and at last have the freedom to explore. That same recognizable damp, rotting, fungal smell of Autumn was around again! I suppose this is the season of fading beauty death and decay, but each year always ends with a tremendous blaze of glory. Think of the beeches on Haldon and on the Exe Valley road from Tiverton to Dunster. We are so lucky to be able to enjoy nature's many annual gifts.

"My sister Emily loved the moors. Flowers brighter than the rose bloomed in the blackest heath for her; out of a sullen hollow in a livid hillside her mind could make an Eden. She found in the bleak solitude many dear delights, and not the least and best loved was liberty"

Charlotte Bronte

NOVEMBER

Nov 1st

England and indeed Britain is still a lovely place. The islands, the coastline, the sea, the wild countryside, the mountains and lakes, the rivers, the variety of people, scenery, weather, opportunities and locations. I wish we could all revere and respect it more.

Today I walked beside the rushing waters of the Dart as they hurled themselves over each other – jostling and tossing for positions – in their hurry to get to the beckoning ocean. Didn't they know that it was prettier and more restful here than on the wide, forever sea? The bronze and gold leaves were above my head and beneath my feet. I wanted to store every beautiful moment.

Nov 6th

I've just returned from a four-day holiday touring mid-England and Wales. Can you imagine the beauty of the quiet leafy lanes and wooded hillsides of the Cotswolds and Shropshire and the vast majestic isolated mountains and valleys of Wales all cloaked in their brown, yellow, orange and red finery and bathed in a golden glow of sunshine under a blue sky? The stillness and reflections of the lakes and estuaries in the early morning haze were glorious. Is it beautiful where you are? I'd love to hear about it.

"In solitude we give passionate attention to our lives, to our memories, to the details around us."

Virginia Woolf

DECEMBER

Dec 7th

Yesterday it snowed. The large feather-sized flakes floated down slowly and unwillingly at first, then in a more determined and bountiful way. Today I drove and walked over the moors to see the spectacle. It was exactly like being in Switzerland and Austria. It was as if the countryside had been decorated for Christmas. The sparkling crisp white crystals lay in their purity all around. The almost bare branches of the trees were edged with white and adorned with silver and green spikes of lichen. The stones had a topping of powdery snow like so many Christmas puddings covered with icing. The robin, the blackbird and the chaffinch flew in and out of the holly tree to pick and feast on its shining red berries. The creatures in the pool were popping to the surface for air and making patterns of concentric circles in the water. Droplets hung on the hazel which already bore small, green, firm catkins in readiness for the New Year and Spring. It was like one giant Christmas card. I was quite happy walking through that silent, wooded beautiful landscape alone, with only the crunch of my footsteps and my thoughts for company.

Dec 14th

I tried to paint some little sprigs of holly, sloe, hawthorn and rose hips together with catkins of alder and hazel in order to make a few Christmas cards. Each one I did got a little better. As always it's a case of try, try and try again!

Dec 24th

My absolute favourite part of Christmas is Christmas Eve. A few days ago I decorated my living room. On the mantelpiece I have artificial holly and red berries, candles and shining baubles. The Christmas tree is aglow with fairy lights and tinsel, on the table in the window. Pale pink tulips and the first bright daffodils add a touch of Spring to the centre of the sideboard and are reflected in the oval mirror. My kitchen windowsill is my indoor garden with pots of purple, white and pink primroses and white scented hyacinths. My father grew Christmas roses and always brought us in a few buds, so in his memory I have placed some on his bureau. He also grew a mass of yellow Winter jasmine so it isn't the perfect Christmas without having a few sprigs of that in a vase. As in the old days I like to bring a bit of the countryside into the house so by my chair I have an arrangement of berries, dried seed heads and ivy. Today I immersed myself in Christmas music and sat quietly by the fire in my warm and pretty cottage listening to the nine lessons and carols from King's College chapel in Cambridge which completed to perfection the peaceful seasonal atmosphere.

Dec 28th

My cousin's wedding anniversary! It won't be long before it is another New Year! I wonder what it will bring? I give thanks for the last one and hope that I may be given the opportunity to continue my travels through Britain and beyond!

For the Beauty of the Earth

For the beauty of the earth
For the beauty of the skies
For the love, which from our birth
Over and around us lies
Lord of all to Thee we raise
This our grateful hymn of praise.

For the beauty of each hour
Of the day and of the night
Hill and vale and tree and flower
Sun and moon and stars of light
Lord of all to Thee we raise
This our grateful hymn of praise.

For the joy of human love
Brother, sister, parent, child
Friends on earth and friends above
Pleasures pure and undefiled
Lord of all to Thee we raise
This our grateful hymn of praise.

Places Visited

Dartington Hall Gardens

Tetbury

Ashprington

Westonbirt

East Cornworthy

Start Point

Dittisham

Mattiscombe

Manaton

Huccaby

Staverton

Kellerton

Torquay

Castle Drogo

Cockington

Drewsteignton

Killerton

Rosemoor

Forde Abbey

Instow

Spitchwick

South Pool

Overbecks, Salcombe

Sunny Cove, East Portlemouth

The Garden House

Paris

Cotehele

Polesden Lacey

Teign Valley
Mottisfont
Dunsford Woods
Barrington Court
Dulverton
Dunkery Beacon
Bicton Gardens
Powderham
Bradford-on-Tone
Meadfoot
Coleton Fishacre
Dartmouth
Greenway House
East Prawle

Mount Edgcumbe
Somerset Levels
Antony
Haldon
Shaldon
Exe Valley
East Lambrook Manor
North Wales
Tintinhull
Montacute
Stourhead
Lacock Abbey
Dartmoor
Exmoor

Dedication

I inherited my love of the natural world and of art and craft from my father, and worked on many of the little paintings in this book whilst in the company of my mother during the latter years of her long life and very much appreciated her unstinting interest, encouragement and praise. In gratitude for their unselfish devotion I dedicate this diary to my beloved parents.